The Messenger

The Messenger

By Jamie Mulgrew

Copyright

Copyright © 2021 by Jamie Mulgrew

All rights reserved. This book or any portion thereof may not be reproduced or used in any manner whatsoever without the publisher's express written permission except for the use of brief quotations in a book review.

Printed in the United States of America by Ingramspark

First Printing October2021

ISBN Print 978-1-7368288-5-4

JEBWizard Publishing

Cranston, RI 02920

www.jebwizardpublishing.com

Dedication

For Aunt Mary Elizabeth Mulgrew

Joan sat down and prayed, "Our Mother, who art in heaven, hallowed be thy name..."

In 2020 amidst a lethal pandemic, amongst dictators and people against science, Joan had secrets she wanted to share with the children of her tribe.

"The first secret," said Joan, "is overcoming the darkness."

If you look hard enough, you will see the light in the dark, which is hope. The more humans embrace the light, the brighter the light becomes.

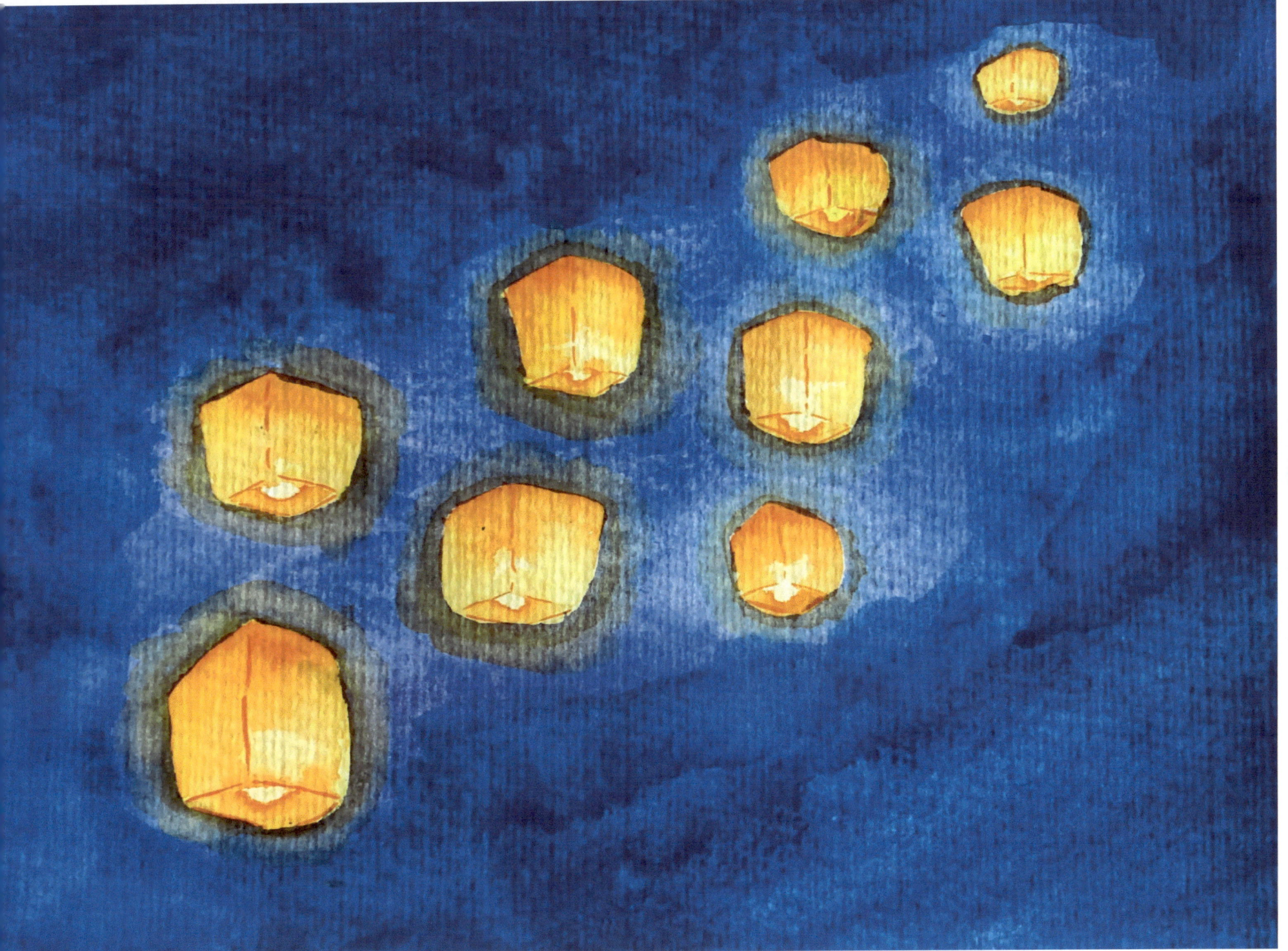

The children asked, "How can we become the light?" "By becoming who we are meant to be," Joan replied.

"How do we do this?".

"By listening to our inner voice."

"How do we listen to our inner voice?" asked the children.

"We can listen to our inner voice when we pray," said Joan.

To pray is to enter the house of the beloved and to feel the spirit of the highest power. To feel the spirit encircle you. To feel the spirit fill you- from the bottom to the top, enveloping your energies, enclosing you. Rising, climbing, and dancing. To be in this power and this power to be in you.

"The second secret is about life."

To live fully is to be free. Free to make your own decisions and to follow your own inner voice. To experience everything that excites you and makes you feel alive inside. To express all your feelings and to defend and protect yourself.

There is a season for everything, winter is as spectacular and beautiful as summer, yet both contain their difficulties.

The world dreamt of you before we met you; you were loved before you were born. Your purpose is within you. To live in harmony is to live out this quest. Only you and you alone can know this secret.

Therefore, you must connect with the power who loves, dreams, and made you. To live out this plan, in body, mind, and soul. Praising your higher power in all you do.

This is the secret to a happy life.

"The third secret is about work, which is prayer in action." To work is to improve the whole, to add value to the community where we live. All work is important if it offers a service to others. We can serve others by teaching, caring, helping, protecting, and inspiring them.

No job is greater or lesser, just as the root of a tree, although unseen, allows the flowers to shine. We should not compare ourselves with others who work, as only you can bring your own gift to the whole. To work is to bring glory to the unseen. When you work with love, you fulfill your purpose.

"The fourth secret is about Evil. Evil seeks to destroy and harm."

We must protect ourselves against the forces of Evil. People who are beaten and bruised can seek to destroy and hurt other people.

When you step back, you can see scars, scabs, and holes. People gripped by Evil are lost. If they work hard to heal, then Evil can cease to exist. The biggest Evil is in people who claim to be from the highest power.

This power never wants to harm or control you. This power only wants to bring peace. The more people hurt other people, the longer and more challenging it is for them to heal.

Through prayer and work, the force of Evil can cease to exist. Through evolution, we can create a world without Evil. We can create a heaven on earth.

"The fifth secret is about pain. Pain allows you to see the truth more clearly."

When you feel pain, however hard, it leaves you healthier and happier. When you choose to not feel pain, life is waiting to be lived again.

To understand is to transform. All transformation is hard, but we can do hard things. Just as the caterpillar becomes a butterfly, you must transform into being even more beautiful and who you are meant to be.

Through pain, we become stronger. To embrace pain is to embrace life. When we accept the purpose of pain and become more fully who we are meant to be, then the pain goes away. If we ignore pain, then the pain grows more severe and harder to embrace.

"The sixth secret is about love. You can only love others as much as you love yourself."

It is hard to love many people; therefore, people choose to love only a few people. We call these people family and friends. Real love helps the other person be the best person they can be. To be the happiest person they can be.

When you love someone, you must let them make their own choices and do what their inner voice tells them to do. Only by sharing the highest power's love can we be in love. Real love encourages, real love forgives. Real love shares all and is found in joy and peace.

Only love is eternal, only love lasts forever. Love does not die. Loving this power and loving other people is the most important thing you can do in life.

"The seventh secret is about the highest power. Male and female, gay and straight, black, and white, we all create this higher power."

Not one of us is less or more worthy than the other. Just closer to the mind of this power if we enter its Mindfulness.

Jesus of Nazareth, Moses, Mohammed of Mecca, Krishna, and Gautama Buddha all connected with this level of awareness.

Jesus of Nazareth died so we could connect with it. Connecting with the highest power is hard to do, but it can be done. It must be done to create heaven on earth.

Joan picked up her bag to go, then stopped to tell the children one more thing.

"We wrote the truth in our hearts. To commit a sin is to deny who we really are. Look deep, deep inside, and you will find, that we are all one.

We are all Gods."

About the Author

Jamie Mulgrew is a former school Principal with a Masters Degree in Education. She is born of Irish parents and was raised in the north of England. Jamie now lives in the USA with her partner Kenzie and is an active member of the episcopal church where she sings in the choir. The Messenger is Jamie's first Children's book. Please follow @themessenger_childrensbook on Instagram and www.themessenger3.godaddysites.com website for updates on upcoming events and resources.

About JEBWizard Publishing

JEBWizard Publishing offers a hybrid approach to publishing. By taking a vested interest in the success of your book, we put our reputation on the line to create and market a quality publication. We offer a customized solution based on your individual project needs.

Our catalog of authors spans the spectrum of fiction, non-fiction, Young Adult, True Crime, Self-help, and Children's books.

Contact us for submission guidelines at

https://www.jebwizardpublishing.com

Info@jebwizardpublishing.com

Or in writing at

JEBWizard Publishing

37 Park Forest Rd.

Cranston, RI 02920

www.ingramcontent.com/pod-product-compliance
Lightning Source LLC
Chambersburg PA
CBHW041108210426

43209CB00063BA/1854